G000075806

To my wonderful Sister

With love from

Other books in this series:
Best Friends
Thank you Mum
Have a Perfect Day
My Dad, My Hero
I've got a crush on you
Stay Calm
Happy Birthday

Published in 2011 by Helen Exley Giftbooks in Great Britain. A copy of the CIP data is available from the British Library on request. All rights reserved. No part of this publication may be reproduced or transmitted in any form or by any means, electronic or mechanical, including photocopy, recording or any information storage and retrieval system without permission in writing from the Publisher.
Printed in China.

Words and illustrations © Jenny Kempe 2011
Design and arrangement © Helen Exley Creative Ltd 2016
The moral right of the author has been asserted.

12 11 10 9 8 7 6 5 4 3

ISBN: 978-1-84634-559-3

Published by HELEN EXLEY®
Helen Exley Giftbooks, 16 Chalk Hill, Watford, Herts WD19 4BG, UK
www.helenexleygiftbooks.com

My Sister

WORDS AND ILLUSTRATIONS BY

JENNY KEMPE

A sister enters
without knocking.
Pries. Spies.
Asks inappropriate questions.
Thinks she knows best.

A sister is an extra
pair of hands.

Your best is good enough
– as long as it is
better than her best.

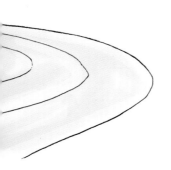

A sister has a way of taking
your stuff without asking.
If enough time elapses
without confrontation,
the stolen goods mysteriously
become her property.

Sisters are confidantes.

Sisters make

a good team.

A sister cajoles, bribes, begs, threatens, nags, runs your personal errands and offers you her dessert for a week.

IF you agree she can borrow your brand-new dress for her Friday night date.

It does not matter how many
hours it is going to take,
if a sister really wants to win.

Sisters are trouble.

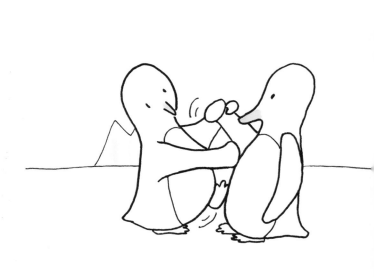

Sisters know how to
make things good again.

Sisters are part of
happy memories.

Sisters show you how
things are done.

A sister is someone
who may give you
the right glove
as a surprise, and the left
for your birthday,
and then ask to borrow
the pair.

A sister is someone
you'll never wish you
were without.

Her triumph is
my triumph.

When you're feeling poorly
others may forget you,
or shy away from you.
Not your sister.

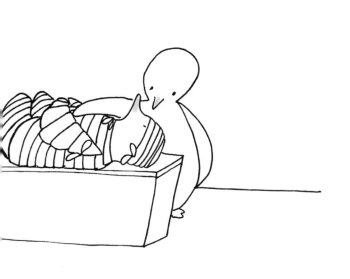

She knows you better than anyone else. She is your history. She is part of what it means to be YOU.

TO MY AMAZING SISTER:
Let's forget about
our differences
– I am incredibly lucky to have
you! You are my sister

...and you mea

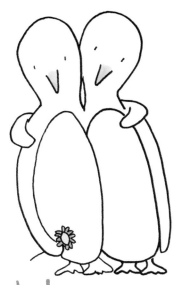

he world to me.

We loved making this book for you.
We hope you'll enjoy the other titles
in our series Life is Beautiful.

The Life is Beautiful Team

About Helen Exley gifts

Our products cover the most powerful range of all human relationships: love between couples, the bonds within families and between friends. No expense is spared in making sure that each book is as thoughtful and meaningful a gift as it is possible to create: good to give, good to receive. You have the result in your hands. If you have loved it — tell others!

Visit our website to see all of Helen Exley's other books and gifts: **www.helenexleygiftbooks.com**

Helen Exley Giftbooks
16 Chalk Hill, Watford, Herts
WD19 4BG, UK
www.helenexleygiftbooks.com